GW00383990

Bunny and Dog

Book 1

The Meeting

Giovanna Gentile

Richard Malthouse

Copyright © 2018 Giovanna Gentile and Richard Malthouse

All rights reserved.

ISBN: 13: 978-1717163554

ISBN-10: 1717163556

DEDICATION

To Luca and Mia

ACTIVITIES

There are various activities to try and these are listed at the back of the book.

An activity is identified by the following butterfly icon

Thanks to Samantha Fleur-Camp for the illustration

ACKNOWLEDGMENTS

We would like to thank the Puppet Company for allowing us to use their products within the illustrations.

The Puppet Company Ltd

Units 2-4 Cam Centre
Wilbury Way
Hitchin
Hertfordshire
SG4 0TW

Telephone +44 (0) 1462 446040

Fax +44 (0) 1462 446041

BUNNY AND DOG

BOOK 1

THE MEETING

Part 1

Dog lived in his house. He liked his house which he thought was a special house for dogs but taller than your average dog house. It was black and very cosy. Dog liked the colour because he was mostly black.

It had a large opening so Dog could look out into the garden.

The dog house was in the garden of a house. Dog was only allowed in the house when the owners were in. But they were not in so Dog was now on duty, he was a guard dog and he took his job very seriously indeed.

In fact, Dog's house was a composter and Dog was totally unaware of this fact. But as he liked it so much that he was allowed to keep it and call it his own.   Dog felt safe in his house, it kept him sheltered from the rain and it was waterproof.

Guarding the house meant that he was always on the lookout for anyone who was not supposed to be there. He was very comfortable in the house and this was because he had a nice comfy bed with green blankets, a red bowl of fresh water and a bone. Dog was never happier than when he was eating a bone.

"I am a very lucky dog" thought Dog as he studied a butterfly that had landed in front of him in the garden.

Dog was looking out of the window one day when he thought he saw something moving at the bottom of the garden, just in the corner of his eye. He stood up as far as he could reach and looked over the garden and to the trees on the other side.

"What was that?" thought Dog. "I will look a little longer and see if I can see anything moving in the garden again" he suggested to himself.

So he sat by the door and looked out into the garden with a great deal of interest. But soon his head was feeling heavy and his eyelids heavier and he soon nodded off.

"Oh dear" said Dog when he woke up, "I fell asleep."

He decided to try again and not go to sleep this time.   This time he decided to stand up so as not to fall asleep. He looked out into the garden with great determination.

But soon his head was feeling heavy and his eyelids heavier and he soon nodded off again.

"Oh dear" said Dog when he woke up, "I fell asleep again, I will never see what is in the garden if I keep falling asleep" he thought.

Dog was determined to stay awake in order to see what was at the bottom of the garden. "I will go outside and hide behind a plant and that way I will stay awake" Said Dog to himself. So he went outside his house and over to a row of flowers.

There he lay right down low and looked towards the end of the garden. He was determined not to go to sleep. Then the sun came out and made Dog very warm. Soon his head was feeling heavy and his eyelids heavier and he soon nodded off behind the flowers.

He woke with a jolt, just in time to see something move at the bottom of the garden. "Aha" said Dog. "Success, I have seen the thing at the bottom of the garden." But Dog was none the wiser as he had no idea what he had seen. He just saw movement and nothing more. "I will have to go down to the bottom of the garden and see what is there" thought Dog.

Dog had decided to go to the bottom of the garden to see what was moving there. He did not know what he was looking for but he felt sure that there was definitely something there and he wanted to find out what. But how was he to go about this?

"I will walk under the very tall flowers" he said to himself. He knew he would not be seen there.

If he ran he might scare whatever was there away. If he just pretended he was going for a walk that may be better.

"I think I will sneak down to the end of the garden and then I will not frighten whatever it is down there away." Thought Dog.

So Dog made his way down the garden. First he hid behind the dustbins, then he moved very carefully along the path.

He stood there for a while, just looking and sniffing the air as dogs do.

Part 2

Dog made his way, very slowly, bit by bit, to the end of the garden.

"Hello" said a voice.

Dog jumped.

There, standing behind Dog was another animal.

Dog turned around and stared at the animal.

"Who and what are you and what are you doing in my garden?" asked Dog with as much authority as he could muster. He realised at this point that he was a little shaken at being discovered and

noted his voice sounded a little too high in pitch.

"Hello, I am Bunny" said Bunny "And you are Dog and you live in the composter over there and you are very fond of sleeping."

Bunny jumped down onto a small brick wall.

How do you know all these things about me?" asked Dog. He suddenly realised what Bunny had said about sleeping. "By the way, I am not that fond of sleeping you know, I am a guard dog."

"Well I saw you sleeping three times today, and that's a fact" said Bunny.

Dog realised that this was indeed true so decided not to dwell on this fact. "You still haven't told me how you know so much about me" he said.

"I keep my eyes and ears open and my mouth shut, you have two eyes, two ears and one mouth and you should use them proportionately" said Bunny.

Dog thought and realised he didn't know what proportionately actually meant. "Bunny" he said "What does proportionately mean?"

"Proportionately in this case means out of your two eyes and two ears and one mouth, you should spend lots of time looking and listening and only a little time talking "

Dog thought he understood.

"So what are you doing in my garden?" Asked Dog.

"Nothing really" said Bunny, "I am just jumping around looking for anything to eat or that I can take back to my burrow."

"What's a burrow?" asked Dog.

"A burrow is where I live and it is underground." She said.

"Wow an underground house that's cool" said Dog. "Can I see it please?"

"Well you are looking at it right now" Said Bunny.

"Where?" said Dog. He looked and looked but could not see a thing.

"There" said Bunny pointing to a patch in the ground, "that is my front door."

"What, that hole?"

"Yes, it is a bit like your door but my version" said Bunny.

"I am tidying today but if you are a good Dog, you are invited to come over for a cup of tea and a muffin" said Bunny.

"Oh yes please" said Dog.

"Then I shall see you at eleven" said Bunny.

Dog had stopped listening and was busy watching a bee on a flower.

"How about eleven?" Repeated Bunny.

"What's eleven?" asked Dog.

"It is a number but I think we can deal with numbers later, I will come and get you tomorrow in the morning before lunch" she said.

Dog agreed and turned to go back to his house.

"Bye Dog" said Bunny.

"Bye Bunny" Said Dog.

Dog was very pleased and went back to his house wagging his tail.

Part 3

Dog woke up the next day and was excited about going to see Bunny in her burrow. He was pleased to have a new friend and he thought it did not matter that Bunny was living in the garden, because she was underground and no one would notice. He waited and waited and waited and then his head was feeling heavy and his eyelids heavier and he soon nodded off.

"Oh dear" said Dog when he woke up, "I fell asleep."

Just then he noticed Bunny jumping up towards him.

"Hi Dog" said Bunny, "did I wake you?"

"I wasn't sleeping I was just thinking with my eyes closed, it helps concentration" said Dog.

"Of course it does" said Bunny who had other ideas.

"Can we go and see your burrow now please" said Dog.

"That's the idea" said Bunny and off she jumped in the direction of her burrow.

"I have been wondering" said Dog, "do you think I will fit in the burrow?"

"I think we are about the same size, so I think you will" said Bunny.

After a short while they were by the entrance to Bunny's burrow.

"I will go first and you follow" said Bunny.

"But how will I know where to go? It will be dark down there" said Dog.

"Trust me on this one" said Bunny and presently disappeared into the burrow.

Dog then held his breath and jumped, head first into the burrow.

To Dog's surprise, he found that contrary to his expectations he could see perfectly in the burrow. This was because Bunny had installed some solar panels which were providing a source of electricity for the lighting. He made his way along the burrow and eventually came to a door. He opened the door and saw a rather large and well-furnished room. Dog looked around and to his amazement saw tables, chairs, a wood-burner stove, books on

shelves, rugs on the floor and any amount of cooking utensils.

"Wow" said Dog.

"Do you like it?" asked Bunny.

"Yes it's brilliant" said Dog.

"How did you get all these things down here through the narrow tunnel?" Asked Dog.

"That is a Bunny secret" said Bunny. "Now how about that tea and muffin, I think it is time for elevenses, what say you?"

In no time at all, Bunny and Dog were sitting in front of the log burner eating muffins and drinking tea.

"Bu-unny?" Said Dog in a way that meant he had a question.

"Ye-es?" said Bunny, in a way that sounded like she was about to answer a question.

"How long have you been here and how is it that we have never met before?"

"I have only recently moved in and the reason you haven't seen me is because I did all the moving in at night and you were fast asleep."

"Oh I see" said Dog. "Bunny, will you tell me about numbers please?" said Dog.

"Of course" said Bunny. "We will learn all about numbers tomorrow."

"Then you are invited to the Dog House tomorrow" said Dog.

They finished their tea and muffins, Dog said goodbye to Bunny, thanking Bunny on a number of occasions. He enjoyed his time with

Bunny and was looking forward to tomorrow already.

Dog made his way to the end of the garden, he was very happy.

Dog arrived at his house he lay down, soon his head was feeling heavy and his eyelids heavier and he soon nodded off and didn't wake up until the following day.

The End

(Until next time)

Activities

Activities for pages 4, 6 and 8:

Adult: To go back to the page to carry out the activity with the child/children

The activity can be chosen to meet the child/children's age and ability.

1. Where is dogs house?

2. Can you remember the colour of Dogs house?

3. What was the house meant to be?

4. Do you have one in your garden?

Activity for page 10:

1. *Can you find and say the first letter sound of each word on the page and say the words?*

   Dog   Bone   Red

2. *When do you think Dog is most happy?*

3. *What colour is Dog's bowl?*

4. *What colour is Dog's blanket?*

5. *Do you think Dog's blanket keeps him warm?*

Activities for pages 10, 12 and 14:

1. *Does Dog stay awake whilst guarding the garden or does he keep falling asleep?*

2. *What else does Dog do?*

3. *Can you find and say the first letter sound of each word on the page and say the words?*

   Saw   Looked   Tree   Far

Activity pages 20 and 22:

1. *Can you remember where Dog fell asleep in the garden?*

2. *Can you find and say the first letter sound of each word on the page and say the word?*

   Garden   Plant   flowers

3. *Can you find the things you have read in the picture?*

Activity pages 26 and 28:

1. *Can you find and say the first letter sound of the words on the page and say the word?*

   Moving Walk Tall Frighten Dustbins

2. *Where does Dog hide in the garden?*

3. *Why does Dog hide?*

4. *What do you think happens next?*

Activity pages 32, 34 and 38:

1. *What animal did Dog find at the bottom of the garden? What do you think happened next?*

2. *Can you find and say the first letter sound of the words on the page and say the word?*

   Animal   Eyes   Ears   Jumped

3. *Can you find the things you have read in the picture?*

Activity Pages 42 and 48:

1. Where does Bunny live?

2. Can you find and say the first letter sound of the words on the

   page and say the word?

   My   Eat   Doing   Jumping

3. Does Bunny invite Dog for tea?

4. What do you think they will eat?

Activity Pages 54, 58 and 62:

1. *Do you think Bunny and Dog are friends?*

2. *Can you find and say the first letter sounds of the words on the page and Say the word?*

    Burrow   Head   Dog   Bunny

3. *Can you find the things you have read in the picture?*

4. *It is dark in the burrow. How does Bunny manage to get light in her house?*

5. *Bunny has chairs and a table in her house, can you think of anything else?*

6. *Do you think Bunny's Burrow is big enough for Dog to go in?*

Activity: Pages 62, 66 and 72:

1. *Look at the pictures; what can you see? Describe what you see.*

2. *What did Bunny and Dog have to eat and drink in Bunny's Burrow?*

3. *What did Bunny have in her house to keep warm?*

4. *What do you think happened next?*

5. *Will Bunny and Dog meet again?*

Extra Activities

1. *Simple Creative activity which also promotes communication and language development.*

You will need:

(Available at any craft shop)

1. *Paper or card, crayons and pencil*

2. *Lollipop stick or straw*

3. *Sellotape or glue and scissors (adult supervision)*

Child/children can draw a picture of Bunny and Dog (adult can help)

Cut the drawn picture (adult supervision and help)

Stick the picture for both Bunny and Dog either on a lollipop stick or straw.

Activity 2:

The child/children can recite their favourite part of the story using the puppets they have made. Enjoy and have fun!

About the Authors

Giovanna Gentile

Giovanna Gentile is an Ofsted registered childcare practitioner. She has a diploma at advanced level in Early learning and childcare and over 30 years' experience. She has cared for over 50 children, past and present and still keeps in contact with those who are now adults and their parents. She is dedicated to ensure that the children achieve the best possible outcome for their age and ability. This is achieved at their own pace in all areas of their development in keeping with the EYFS and every child matters. She seeks to ensure that the children are able to make a positive contribution as they grow and make a smooth transition into school and later as adults. She has two daughters and two wonderful grandchildren Luca and Mia.

Dr Richard Malthouse

Dr Richard Malthouse is Senior Lecturer on the BA (Hons) Education Studies programme at the University of East London. He currently lectures in Education with Psychology and engages in seminars with Early Years students. Prior to this, he worked at the University of West London and as a Teaching Fellow at Brunel University, lecturing on the BA in Contemporary Education. He is currently researching elements of metacognition and the transition from Level 3 to 4 and is developing a new model of reflective practice aimed at Year 1 students.

Links to the Early Years Foundation Stage (EYFS)

1.5. Educational programmes must involve activities and experiences for children, as follows:

• Communication and language development involves giving children opportunities to experience a rich language environment; to develop their confidence and skills in expressing themselves; and to speak and listen in a range of situations

• Literacy development involves encouraging children to link sounds and letters and to begin to read and write. Children must be given access to a wide range of reading materials (books, poems, and other written materials) to ignite their interest

• Understanding the world involves guiding children to make sense of their physical world and their community through opportunities to explore, observe and find out about people, places, technology and the environment .

1.7. For children whose home language is not English, providers must take reasonable steps to provide opportunities for children to develop and use their home language in play and learning, supporting their language development at home. Providers must also ensure that children have sufficient opportunities to learn and reach a good standard in English language during the EYFS: ensuring children are ready to benefit from the opportunities available to them when they begin Year 1. When assessing communication, language and literacy skills, practitioners must assess children's skills in English. If a child does not have a strong grasp of English language, practitioners must explore the child's skills in the home language with parents and/or carers, to establish whether there is cause for concern about language delay.

This publication will also available in a range of languages, as a dual-language story, to assist those whose home language is not English.

The early learning goals includes a number of 'prime areas'. The most relevant of which, for this publication is:

Communication and language. Listening and attention: children listen attentively in a range of situations. They listen to stories, accurately anticipating key events and respond to what they hear with relevant comments, questions or actions. They pay attention to what others say and respond appropriately, while engaged in another activity.

Department of Education (2017) Early Years Foundation Stage. Available online at:

https://www.foundationyears.org.uk/files/2017/03/EYFS_STATUTORY_FRAMEWORK_2017.pdf

Flutter by butterfly

37655947R00055

Printed in Great Britain
by Amazon